CRIM VOCABULARY IN USE

Master 400+ Essential Criminal Law Terms And Phrases Explained With Examples In 10 Minutes A Day

JOHNNY CHUONG

ISBN: 9781976712531

TABLE OF CONTENT

INTRODUCTION

Thank you and congratulate you for downloading the book *"Criminal Law Vocabulary In Use: Master 400+ Essential Criminal Law Terms And Phrases Explained With Examples In 10 Minutes A Day."*

With a clear, concise, and engaging writing style, Johnny Chuong will provides you over 400 criminal law terms and phrases that help you expand your legal words list with a practical understanding of criminal law topics such as *types of crimes, definitions of complicity, types of criminal punishments, sentences, judicial measures, aggravating factors, mitigating factors, probation, exemption of punishment, defendants, plaintiffs, trials, criminal procedures* **and much much more**. If you'd like to increase your wide range of legal vocabulary as well as enhance your knowledge of criminal law and criminal procedure, then this book may be the most important book that you will ever read.

As the author of the book, Johnny Chuong promises this book will be an invaluable source of legal reference for professionals, international lawyers, law students, criminal professionals and anyone else who want to improve their use of legal terminology, succinct clarification of legal terms and have a better understanding of criminal law and criminal procedure. This book provides you with a comprehensive and highly practical approach in legal contexts, the world of criminal law related to criminals, punishments, investigation, procuration, trials, defense, and other procedural aspects of criminal law. All legal terms and phrases are well written and explained clearly in plain English.

Take action today and start mastering 400+ essential criminal law terms and phrases explained with examples tomorrow!

Thank you again for purchasing this book, and I hope you enjoy it.

ESSENTIAL CRIMINAL LAW PHRASES AND TERMS

SECTION A

A criminal offence: an act that is punished by law;

The Criminal Code applies to every criminal offence committed within the country.

All organizations that commit criminal offences are equal before the law regardless of the type of business and economic sector.

A gangster: a member of an organized group of violent criminals.

He is a gangster who shot five bystanders and kidnapped a woman.

A criminal record: a list of crimes that a person has committed.

That the offender commits a less serious crime and does not have prior criminal record may be considered a mitigating factor.

An attempt to commit a crime: means an intent and conduct towards completion of a crime that does not occur for reasons not intended by the criminal.

Any person who commits an unsuccessful crime has to bear criminal responsibility.

An accomplice: someone who helps another commit a crime.

He got a life imprisonment sentence for being an accomplice to murder.

The gun killer of the president had a gang of accomplices who were involved with the crime.

A general amnesty: an official pardon extended by the government to a group of people who have been convicted of political offences.

A general amnesty is granted the offender who has a fatal disease during the process of investigation, prosecution or trial and no longer poses a threat to society.

A fatal disease: a disease that causes death.

A criminal offender might be exempt from criminal responsibility if she/he has a fatal disease during the process of investigation, prosecution or trial and no longer poses a threat to society.

A natural disaster: a natural event such as a flood, tornadoes, earthquake, or hurricane that causes a lot of damage and kills many people.

Thousands of people died in the natural disaster.

Administrative penalty: a monetary penalty, or fine.

A fine might be imposed as an administrative penalty upon an offender.

The offender has incurred an administrative penalty for the appropriation of property.

A consanguineous relationship: a relationship between persons who have the same ancestry or descent.

Any person who has sexual intercourse with another person in the knowledge that he/she is in a consanguineous relationship, a sibling or half-sibling shall face a penalty of 02 - 07 years of imprisonment.

A professional manner: to behave professionally.

The offence is committed in a professional manner.

A disciplinary penalty: a penalty concerning or enforcing discipline.

The offender has incurred a disciplinary penalty for the same offence.

Afforestation land: land that is used for planting trees in order to make a forest.

Permitting illegal repurposing of forest or afforestation land.

Appropriation: the action of taking something for your own use, usually without the owner's permission.

Appropriation of narcotic substances.

Any person who appropriates narcotic substances shall face a penalty of 02 - 04 years of imprisonment.

Appropriation of property using a computer network, telecommunications network or electronic device.

An unqualified person: a person who does not have the qualifications needed for a particular task.

Allowing an unqualified person to operate a vehicle on public roads.

Appropriation, trading, destruction of an organization's seal or document.

Any person who appropriates, sells, buys or illegally destroys an organization's seal or document shall face a penalty of up to 02 years of imprisonment.

Abuse of power or position for appropriation of property.

Any person who abuses his/her position or power to appropriate another person's property shall face a penalty of 01 - 05 years' imprisonment.

Abuse of power or position to influence another person for personal gain.

Any person who abuses his position or power to directly request, receive or promise to receive money, property or other tangible benefits in order to influence an office-holder to perform or not to perform certain tasks shall face a penalty of 02 - 05 years of imprisonment.

A broker: a person who acts as an intermediary.

To broker: to act as an agent for others.

Brokering bribery.

Any person who brokers a bribery that is money, property or other tangible benefits shall face a penalty of 03 years of imprisonment.

Attendees in court: persons who attend in court.

Civil defendants are entitled to attend the trial; provide opinions, request the Court president to question attendees in court.

Abuse of influence over an office holder for personal gain.

Any person who directly or through an intermediary receives money, property or other tangible benefits in order to use his/her influence over an office-holder to urge him/her to perform or not to perform certain tasks shall face a penalty of up to 03 years imprisonment.

An innocent person = a guiltless person: a person who does not do crime or anything related to that/ a person who is not guilty of a particular crime.

Any competent person who brings a criminal prosecution against an innocent person shall face a penalty of up to 05 years of imprisonment.

The offence results in a wrongful conviction of an innocent person for a serious crime.

A guilty person: a person has committed an offense, crime.

Failure to bring a criminal prosecution against a guilty person.

A judicial officer: an officer of the court (usually a judge or magistrate) who makes a decision.

Any person who abuses their position or power to force a judicial officer to act against the law and as a result infringes upon the lawful rights and interests of the individual shall face a penalty of up to 03 years of imprisonment.

Abduction: the action of forcibly taking someone away against his/her will, usually by using violence, threatening to use violence, or deceiving.

The abduction of a person under 16.

Abuse of trust to appropriate property.

Any person who takes a loan, borrows, leases property of another person or receives property of another person under a contract, then uses deception to appropriate it or refuses to repay the loan or return the property when the repayment or return of property is due despite he/she is capable of doing so shall face a penalty of up to 03 years of imprisonment.

Assault: a violent physical attack.

To assault: to attack someone violently.

Assaulting companions.

Any person who deliberately attacks his/her companion violently at work shall face a penalty of up to 02 years of imprisonment.

Adjudication: the act of a court in making a judicial ruling, a judgment or a decision.

The processing of filing of charges, investigation, prosecution and adjudication shall abide by the procedures and formalities as defined by law.

An unjust conviction: a conviction that is not morally right and fair.

To protect guiltless people from an unjust conviction.

Accused persons: persons who have been arrested for or formally charged with a criminal offense.

Accused persons include detainees, suspects, defendants.

An accused person is entitled to but is not obliged to prove his innocence.

An interpreter: a person who translates oral or written language (usually the testimony of a witness) into another language.

A translator: a person who has the right to carry out authorised translations/ a person who translates speech.

Request or recommend the designation and replacement of defense counsels, interpreters and translators.

A valuator: a person who estimates the value of objects, property.

Valuators are entitled to study case files in connection with the subjects of valuation; refuse to perform activities of valuation without adequate time for relevant tasks.

Request valuation, revaluation of property and change of valuators.

A witness = a testifier: a person who gives testimony or evidence in a court of law.

Witnesses are entitled to read reports of legal proceedings, and give opinions on legal proceedings that they witness.

An investigator: a person who is assigned to file charges and investigate criminal cases.

Investigators have duties and authority to directly inspect, verify and document criminal information.

Investigators, before inquiring into the case, must ask about the relationship of the witness testifiers, suspects and defendants.

A defendant: a person who is accused or charged of committing an offense.

Defendants are entitled to defend themselves or be defended.

The rights and duties of defendants as suspects are executed by their legal representatives.

A first-instance court = court of first instance: a court in which legal proceedings are first heard.

A first-instance Court's judgments or rulings may be appealed according to the Law.

An appellate court = court of appeals: a court that has the power to review and overturn decisions made by lower courts.

The first-instance Court's judgment, verdict or decision shall be reheard by an appellate Court if appealed.

A trial panel of an appellate Court shall comprise three judges.

An appellate court shall review the content of sentences and rulings being appealed.

Amendments: The correction of an error committed in any process, or proceeding at law.

Amendments to the decision on pressing charges against suspects.

Abolishment = put an end to.

Abolishment of unfounded and illegal decisions.

Accusation: the action of making a charge against a person who is guilty of an offense that is punishable.

Procedures, formalities, and authority for the settlement of complaints and accusations are governed by law.

Defenders of legitimate rights and benefits of persons facing accusations are sought by individuals accused to protect their legitimate rights and benefits.

A misdemeanor: a less serious crime.

In flagrante = red-handed: someone is being discovered in or just after the act of committing a crime.

Conducting criminal proceedings against perpetrators of misdemeanors in flagrante.

Persons held in emergency custody or arrested for criminal acts in flagrante are entitled to be informed of reasons of their temporary detainment and arrest.

A suspect: a person who is accused or suspected of committing a crime and being under investigation by law enforcement officials.

Investigation officers have the duties and authority to interrogate suspects.

A denouncer: a person who accuses or informs against someone else publicly.

Investigation officers have the duties and authority to obtain statements from denouncers.

An informant: a person who provides information about criminal activities to a competent agency.

Denouncers, informants, and entities reporting a crime are entitled to be informed of the final settlement of denunciations, information and requisitions.

A legal assistance: a legal support staff member (not a lawyer) who has an advanced understanding of the law and legal proceedings, after education and training, performed substantive legal tasks.

A governmental legal aid center appoints a legal assistant or lawyer to defend persons qualified for legal aid.

A solicitor: a person who is trained to prepare legal documents and give advice on legal subjects and can represent clients in a lower court.

A solicitor providing legal aid must present the letter of appointment by legal aid providers and his lawyer registration card.

A bar association: a professional institution of lawyers/ an association or a group of attorneys.

A bar association assigns a law firm to appoint defense counsel(s).

Attestation: the act of giving testimony or evidence that something is true, genuine, or authentic.

Attestation in criminal lawsuits.

Acquisition: the process of getting or collecting something.

Acquisition of exhibits.

Exhibits must be acquired promptly and fully and their actual conditions must be described precisely in writing and in case files.

Autopsy: A medical examination of a body after death by a forensic autopsy expert in order to determine the cause of death.

Forensic post-mortem expert witnesses shall conduct an autopsy under the management of investigators.

An autopsy shall require witnesses.

Appeal: To ask a more senior court to review a decision or verdict of a subordinate court.

Right to appeal.

Crime victims, defendants, and their representatives shall have the right to appeal against the judgments or rulings of the first instance court.

An accomplice: an accomplice means an organizer, perpetrator, instigator or abettor.

The accomplice will not take criminal responsibility for unjustified force used by the perpetrator.

Aggravating factors: factors that make an offense more serious/ factors that can cause punishment to increase.

The following circumstances are considered aggravating factors:

a) The crime is committed in a professional manner;

b) The crime is of a gangster-like nature;

c) The offender is determined to commit the crime to the end;

d) Recidivism or dangerous recidivism;

SECTION B

Banned commodities: items are banned or restricted for carriage on by the law.

Manufacture or trading of banned commodities.

Possession or transport of banned commodities.

Possession, transport of banned goods.

Manufacturing and trading of banned goods.

Bribe taker: a person who receives a sum of money, presents, or something valuable that someone offers to do something for him/her.

Bribe giver: a person who offers or gives to another a sum of money or something valuable in order to persuade him or her to do something.

Any person who abuses his/her power to directly receive a sum of money, presents, or something valuable to act or not to act in the interests of or at the request of the bribe giver shall face a penalty of 02 - 05 years of imprisonment.

Breach of duty: a failure to do something that someone is legally responsible for.

Any person who injures himself or uses other deceitful methods to evade discharging his duties shall face a penalty of up to 02 years of imprisonment.

Bail = surety: money or valuable collateral that is paid to the court as a deposit of a security that the arrested person will appear in court when his/her case goes to trial.

Presiding judges are entitled to make decisions on bail.

The length of bail time shall not exceed the time of investigation, prosecution or adjudication.

Surety is a preventive measure in lieu of detention.

SECTION C

Criminal Code

The Criminal Code is meant to protect security, human rights, citizenship rights, the equality among ethnic groups, the interests of the State, punish crimes and raise people's awareness of compliance with the law.

No one has to incur criminal liability if he or she does not commit a criminal offence that is regulated by the Criminal Code.

Citizenship rights

A person who is sentenced to imprisonment for infringement of national security shall be derived some of the citizenship rights such as the right to work in regulatory agencies and serve in the people's army.

Commit criminal offences: to do something illegal.

All individuals that commit criminal offences are equal before the law.

Criminals: a person who commits a crime.

All criminals are equal before the law regardless of ethnicity, gender, religion, belief, social class or social status.

Complicity: complicity is a situation in which two or more people deliberately commit the same crime.

They are guilty of complicity in the murder.

There is an evident complicity between the two men.

Criminal prosecution: the conduct of legal proceedings against a defendant for his or her criminal behavior.

Time limit for criminal prosecution.

Failure to bring a criminal prosecution against a guilty person.

Complicity: complicity is a situation in which two or more people deliberately commit the same crime.

He is suspected of complicity in the fraud.

Concealment of crimes: the act of concealing the traces or exhibits of the crime without prior promises.

Any person who conceals the traces or exhibits of the crime or commits other acts that obstruct the discovery, investigation shall bear criminal responsibility for concealment of crimes.

Community sentence: a sentence whereby an offender is ordered to work in the community instead of going to prison.

Community sentence shall be imposed upon people who commit less serious crimes, have stable jobs or fixed residences and do not have to be isolated from society.

Confiscation of property: confiscation of property means confiscation and transfer of part of or all of the property under the ownership of the convict to the state budget.

Confiscation of money and items directly related to the crime.

Corruption-related crimes: crimes that typically involves bribery.

Death sentence shall be imposed upon persons who commit corruption-related crimes.

Commutation: the act of changing a judicial sentence to another one that is less severe.

Commutation of sentence.

Commutation under special circumstances.

Counterfeit: made in exact imitation of something with the intention to deceive or defraud.

Manufacture or trading of counterfeit foods, foodstuff or food additives.

Production, possession, transport of counterfeit money.

Causing environmental pollution: Burying, dumping or discharging hazardous wastes or persistent organic pollutants into the environment.

Chemicals, garbage, and waste water are the most common pollutants causing environmental pollution.

Coercing suicide: the act of cruelly treating, frequently oppressing, abusing or humiliating someone to such an extent that such person commits suicide.

Any person who frequently oppresses, cruelly treats, abuses or humiliates his/her care-dependent to such an extent that such person commits suicide shall face a penalty of 02 - 05 years of imprisonment.

Coercive labor: the act of using violence, threat of violence or otherwise forces a person to work against his/her will.

Any person who transfers or receives someone under 16 for sexual slavery, coercive labor, or taking body parts shall face a penalty of 12 years' imprisonment.

Coca plants: plants whose leaves contain cocaine and other alkaloids.

Narcotic substances: substances such as opium or heroin that affect mood or behavior, especially illegal ones.

Any person who grows opium poppy plants, cannabis plants, coca plants, or other plants containing narcotic substances shall face a penalty of 05 years of imprisonment.

Conviction: a formal declaration that someone is guilty of a particular crime.

An unspent conviction.

A wrongful conviction.

Concealment of illegal use of narcotic substances.

Any person who conceals the illegal use of narcotic substances shall face a penalty of up to 07 years of imprisonment.

Conscription: compulsory enrollment of persons into the armed forces.

Avoiding conscription.

Any person who fails to comply with regulations of law on conscription, defies an enlistment order or military training order shall face a penalty of up to 02 years of imprisonment.

Classified information: secret information that requires protection of confidentiality.

Criminal impersonation: the action of assuming a false position or rank to commit illegal acts.

Any person who assumes a false position or rank to commit illegal acts other than the appropriation of property shall face a penalty of up to 02 years of imprisonment.

Charge: A formal accusation of an offense.

Filing: the action of filing documents.

Filing of charges against suspects.

When a person is found to commit a crime, investigation authorities shall decide to file charges against suspects.

Combat crime: to fight against crime.

A variety of measures and actions taken by the forces of the law to combat crime.

Confession: A voluntary admission of guilt made by a person charged with the commission of a crime.

A perpetrator's confession.

He confessed to stealing the money.

Coercive delivery: the competent authorities' compulsion of the attendance of persons who are held in emergency custody or temporarily detained.

Coercive delivery may apply to persons held in emergency custody or facing charges.

Custody: The state of keeping someone for inspection, investigation or security.

Complaint: the first written document filed with the court by someone who claims legal rights against another.

A complaint filing must be accompanied by a filing fee payable to the court clerk.

Persons filing complaints shall be entitled to obtain the decision to process complaints.

Criminal charge: an official accusation made by a competent authority asserting that someone has committed a criminal offense.

Any person who violates legal regulations on arrest, imprisonment, custody, charge shall face criminal charges according to the laws.

Authority to press criminal charges.

The decision to press criminal charges.

Captivity: the state of being kept or held.

Detention facility holding the suspect or defendant in captivity.

Crime victim: someone who has become a victim of a particular crime.

Crime victims are persons who suffer from direct damage to physical body, mentality and property.

Civil plaintiff: the party who initiates a lawsuit against another in a court of law.

Civil plaintiffs are persons and organizations suffering from damage caused by criminal acts and filing damage claim.

Civil plaintiffs are entitled to defend or have their legitimate rights and benefits defended.

Civil defendant: a person or an organization that is sued in a court of law.

Civil defendants are persons who incur liabilities for compensations according to the laws.

Civil defendants are entitled to appeal against the Court's judgments and rulings on compensations.

Case file: a collection of evidence and documents relating to a particular criminal case.

Read, transcribe and photocopy documents from case files.

The defense counsel has the right to read, transcribe and photocopy documents from case files for activities of pleading upon the end of investigations.

Criminal lawsuits = Criminal cases.

Competent procedural authorities, when investing, prosecuting and hearing criminal lawsuits must attest the existence of the crime, time, space and facts of the crime.

Confrontation: cross-examine witnesses in order to challenge their testimony.

If testimonies from two or more people come into conflict in spite of various investigative measures implemented, investigators shall conduct a confrontation.

Crime scene examination: an examination of a location where an illegal act took place.

An examination of crime scenes requires the presence of witnesses.

Investigators organize the examination of the scenes where crimes take place to seek criminal traces, evidences, items and relevant documents.

Case suspension: A temporary stop of a case.

The presiding judge shall decide to suspend a case if the location of a suspect or defendant is unknown despite the expiration of the time limit for trial preparation.

If there are several defendants or suspects in one case but the reason for case suspension does not apply to all of them, the lawsuit shall be suspended for each defendant or suspect separately.

Case dismissal: The termination of a criminal case by a judge.

The presiding judge shall decide to dismiss a case if the procuracy revokes all decisions to prosecute before the trial begins.

Case resumption: the act of restarting; recommencement; reopening of a case.

If the prescriptive period for criminal prosecution is still effective and there are grounds to annul the decision to suspend or dismiss a case, the Presiding judge issuing such decision shall decide to resume the case.

The decision to resume the case must specify reasons for case resumption.

Conciliation = mediation: the action of mediating between parties.

The remedy of community conciliation.

A decision to implement the remedy of community conciliation shall have reasons and grounds of the decision, time and location of the conciliation.

SECTION D

Deceitful: not honest; deceptive, misleading.

The offender employs deceitful methods to commit the offense.

Criminal offenses committed by deceitful methods shall be strictly punished.

Deliberate crime: The offender is aware of the danger of his/her act to society, foresees consequences of such act and wants such consequences to happen.

He committed a deliberate crime while he had been conditionally released.

Disruption = interruption.

Obstruction or disruption of a computer network, a telecommunications network or electronic devices.

Disruption in court.

Disruption of security: the act of inciting, persuading, gathering other people to disrupt security for the purpose of opposing the people's government.

Any person who, for the purpose of opposing the people's government, incites, persuades, gathers other people to disrupt security shall face a penalty of 05 - 15 years of imprisonment.

Disruption of detention facility: the act of causing disruption at a detention facility, assisting other people to escape from a detention facility for the purpose of opposing the people's government.

Disturbing the peace: to interrupt the peace.

The police arrested him for disturbing the peace.

Determinate imprisonment: the act or process of forcing the convict to serve his/her sentence in a jail or prison over a certain period of time.

Determinate imprisonment shall not be imposed upon a person who commits a less serious crime for the first time and has a fixed residence.

Death sentence: a judge's official statement ordering a convicted defendant to be punished by death.

Death sentence is imposed upon persons committing extremely serious crimes that infringe national security, human life, and drug-related crimes.

Deprivation: the state of being deprived.

Deprivation of certain citizenship rights.

Deliberate disclosure of classified information.

Any person who deliberately discloses or deals in classified information shall face a penalty of up to 07 years of imprisonment.

Denouncement: the action of accusing or informing against someone publicly.

Drug-related crimes: crimes that illegal drugs are related to in multiple ways.

Confiscation of property shall only be imposed upon people who are convicted of drug-related crimes.

Destruction: the act of destroying something.

Destruction of works, facilities, vehicles important to national security.

Expropriation or destruction shall be applied to instruments, vehicles used for the commission of the crime.

Destruction of aquatic resources.

Any person who uses poisons, explosives, electricity, banned fishing equipment or other chemicals for fishing or destructing aquatic resources shall face a penalty of up to 03 years of imprisonment.

Despicable motives: very unpleasant or bad feelings.

The offense is committed by despicable motives.

Disturbance: the interruption of a settled and peaceful condition.

Public order crime: criminal acts that are considered as harmful to the public good and moral values.

Disturbance of public order.

Any person who causes disturbance of public order which negatively impacts social safety, order or security shall face a penalty of up to 02 years of imprisonment.

Detention: the act of detaining or holding someone in custody.

Temporary detention.

The duration of temporary detention shall be deducted from the duration of a community sentence.

Illegally releasing a person under arrest, a person held in temporary detention or a prisoner.

Held in detention.

Distrained property: property that are seized and held to compel payment as of debts.

Using, transferring, swapping, hiding or destroying distrained property.

Deliberate destruction of property.

Any person who deliberately destroys another person's property shall be liable to a fine or face a penalty of up to 03 years of imprisonment.

Desertion: the action of illegally leaving the armed forces.

Any person who leaves the armed forces without permission shall face a penalty of up to 03 years of imprisonment.

Disclosure: *the action of revealing something.*

Deliberate disclosure of military secrets.

Any person who deliberately discloses military secrets shall face a penalty of 05 years of imprisonment.

Double jeopardy: the prosecution or trial of a person for the same offense that he or she has already been acquitted.

A person is not charged, investigated, prosecuted or tried on an act, for which a Court's effective conviction has been passed.

Defense counsel: a trial lawyer who is the defendant's representative.

Defense counsels of accused persons.

Defense counsels are entitled to meet and inquire about persons facing charges; gather and present evidences, documents, items and request.

Distrainment of property: the action of seizing and holding property to compel payment or reparation, as of debts.

Distrainment of property applies to suspects and defendants to guarantee compensations over damage.

Distrainment of property must be done in the presence of suspects or defendants or their representatives.

Detainee: someone who is held in custody, usually for criminal reasons.

Accused persons include detainees, suspects, defendants, and those who are arrested.

Deterioration: the action or process of becoming diminished or impaired in quality, character, or value.

Evident materials must be preserved intact and protected from loss, disorder, and deterioration.

Deposition: the testimony of a witness under oath.

Deposition by witness testifiers.

Deposition by crime victims.

Deposition by civil plaintiffs and civil defendants.

Discharge: the act of releasing someone.

Discharge of defendants.

The presiding judge must declare the immediate discharge, in the courtroom, of a defendant in detention, if he/she is guiltless; or he/she is exempt from criminal liabilities or penalties.

Death penalty = capital punishment: A sentence of death imposed upon a convicted criminal.

Procedures for the review of the death penalty before execution.

A death penalty shall be executed if the President of the Supreme Court does not appeal through reopening or cassation procedures.

SECTION E

Express contrition: the state of feeling remorseful or sorry for committing a crime.

Leniency shall be applied to criminals who show cooperative attitudes; inform on accomplices; express contrition, and voluntarily compensate for damage they inflict;

That the offender expresses cooperative attitude or contrition may be considered a mitigating factor.

Expropriation: the action of expropriating; the act of taking the property of the private owner for public use or benefit by the state or an authority.

Expropriation shall be applied to illegal profits earned from the commission of the crime.

Extremely serious crime: Extremely serious crime means a crime whose danger to society is enormous and for which the maximum sentence of the bracket is life imprisonment or death.

Confiscation of property shall be imposed upon people who are convicted of extremely serious crimes against national security, drug-related crimes, or corruption.

Espionage: the act of spying or of using spies to obtain political and other secret information of a nation.

Any person who commits espionage shall face a penalty of 11 - 18 years of imprisonment, life imprisonment or death.

Embezzlement: someone who abuses his/her position or power to embezzle property under his/her management assessed.

He is sentenced to death for embezzlement.

Expulsion: a sentenced foreigner is forced to leave the territory of a particular country where he/she committed the crime.

Expulsion shall not be combined with other sentences.

Expungement: The process by which the record of a criminal conviction is eliminated.

Conviction expungement under a court's decision.

Expungement of criminal records.

Expungement of conviction.

Evasion: the act of deliberately avoiding something.

Evasion of social insurance, health insurance, unemployment insurance payment for employees.

Exemption of punishment.

The offender may be exempt from punishment after the damage has been repaired and compensation has been paid.

Epidemic: a widespread occurrence of an infectious disease in a community or region during a given time period.

The offender takes advantage of a natural disaster or epidemic to commit the offense.

Establishing illegal funds: the action of abusing the position or power to establish a fund against the law and the use of such fund results in damage state property.

Any person who abuses his/her position or power to establish a fund against the law and the use of such fund results in damage state property shall face a penalty of up to 05 years of imprisonment.

Extraction: the act of extracting something.

Offences against regulations on extraction and protection of forests and forest product management.

Endangered animals: animals that are in danger of disappearing forever.

Rare animals: animals that are not common or very unusual.

Illegal hunting, killing, raising, imparking, transporting, trading of endangered, rare animals.

Emergency custody: Emergency custody of a person is permitted when there are substantial evidences that such person is going to commit a horrific or extremely severe felony.

The order for emergency custody must specify full name and address of the detainee, reason and grounds for detainment.

Expert witness: a person who has knowledge beyond that of the ordinary person. Their opinion can be helpful in problem solving.

Change or request for replacement of expert witnesses.

Evidence: proof of fact(s) presented at a court of law.

A legal representative of a juridical person shall be entitled to present evidences, documents, items and requests.

Verification and collection of evidences, documents and items.

Evident materials = Exhibits: things include means and tools of crimes, objects with criminal traces, criminals' targets, money or other items as satisfactory evidences of criminal offenses.

Intact: something that is complete and that must not be damaged in any situation.

Exhibits/ Evident materials must be preserved intact and protected from loss, disorder and deterioration.

Electronic data: Electronic data is composed of letters, signals, images, numbers, sound or similar elements created, stored and transmitted through electronic media.

Electronic data is collected through computer networks, electronic media, telecommunication networks and other electronic sources.

SECTION F

Fine: an amount of money that is ordered to be paid, as a punishment in a criminal case.

Fine is imposed as a primary sentence against people who commit less serious crimes or serious crimes.

Fraud: a person who intends to deceive others/ the crime of getting money by deceiving others.

Obtaining property by fraud.

Commission of frauds in insurance business.

Falsification of election or referendum result: the act of making false the result of an election or referendum.

Any person who falsifies the election or referendum result shall face a penalty of up to 02 years of imprisonment.

Freedom of speech: the legal right to freely express someone's opinions.

Infringement upon freedom of speech.

Freedom of the press: the right to publish newspapers, magazines, and other printed papers.

Any person who abuses the freedom of the press, freedom of speech, freedom of religion to infringe upon the interests of the State, lawful rights and interests of citizens shall face a penalty of up to 02 years of community sentence.

False advertising: the use of misleading, or false information to advertise goods or services to consumers.

Any person who falsely advertises his/her goods or services shall face a penalty of up to 03 years of community sentence.

Forest destruction.

Any person who sets fire or destroys forests shall face a penalty of up to 03 years of imprisonment.

Facilitation: the act of making an activity easy or easier.

Facilitation of illegal use of narcotic substances.

Any person who facilitates the use of narcotic substances in any form shall face a penalty of up to 05 years of imprisonment.

Flammable substances: substances that are easily set on fire.

Toxic substances: substances that are poisonous.

Offences against regulations of law on the management of flammable substances and toxic substances.

Forced prostitution = involuntary prostitution: prostitution that occurs as a result of coercion.

Forced prostitution that results in the victim's death or suicide.

To fabricate: to invent or produce something false for the purpose of deception.

Fabricating an organization's seal or documents and use thereof.

Any person who fabricates an organization's seal or document or use it to commit an illegal act shall face a penalty of up to 03 years of imprisonment.

To falsify: to change something, such as a document for the purpose of deception.

Falsifying information in the request for indemnity or insurance payout.

Fabricating a document or issuing a fabricated document;

Forging an office holder's signature.

Falsification: the action of falsifying information of something for the purpose of deception.

Falsification of case files.

Any judicial officer who falsifies, swaps, destroys or damages documents or evidence of the case shall face a penalty of up to 05 years of imprisonment.

Forcible sexual intercourse.

Any person who employs trickery to make another person who is his care-dependent or a person in extreme need to reluctantly have sexual intercourse or other sexual activities shall face a penalty of up to 10 years of imprisonment.

Sexual intercourse: the physical act of sex between two people.

Fraud: the action of getting money by deceiving people.

Obtaining property by fraud.

A person who uses deception to obtain another person's property shall face a penalty of up to 03 years of imprisonment.

Forced escort: the act of coercively taking witness testifiers, persons denounced or facing requisitions for charges to a place of investigation, prosecution or adjudication.

Forced escort may apply to witness testifiers absent despite of subpoenas not due to force majeure or objective obstacle.

Freezing of accounts: the action of freezing the accounts of a defendant in order to prevent him/her withdrawing money.

Freezing of account means the transactions in such account cannot be performed until further notice.

SECTION G

Grave: a hole dug in the ground where a dead person is buried.

Remains: a dead body; corpse.

Infringement upon human bodies, graves or remains.

Any person who commits grave robbery or otherwise infringes upon a dead body, grave or human remains shall face a penalty of up to 03 years of imprisonment.

Gambling: the activity of betting money at a game.

Illegal gambling

Any person who illegally gambles in any shape or form with the stakes (in cash or kind) shall face a penalty of up to 02 year's imprisonment.

Gambling den: a place where people meet to engage in illegal gambling.

Organizing gambling or running gambling-dens.

Any person who organizes gambling or runs a gambling den shall face a penalty of up to 05 years of imprisonment.

Giving bribes.

Any person who directly or through an intermediary gives or promises to give money, property or other tangible benefits to an office holder or another person in order to influence him/her to perform or not to perform certain tasks in the interests of the bribe giver shall face a penalty of up to 03 years of imprisonment.

SECTION H

Human rights

Criminal procedure code is intended to defend human rights and citizenship rights, to expose and settle every criminal act in precise, just and timely manners, to protect the legitimate rights and interests of individuals and organizations, to educate people to consciously conform to the laws.

Human trafficking: the action of using violence, threatening to use violence to illegally transport people from one country or area to another, usually for the purposes of forced labour, taking body parts or commercial sexual exploitation.

There are various forms of human trafficking, including sexual exploitation and labour exploitation.

Trafficking of people under 16 years of age.

High treason: someone colludes with foreign entities in infringing the independence, sovereignty and territorial integrity of their own nation.

A person who prepares for high treason crimes shall bear criminal responsibility.

He was exiled to an island for the crime of high treason.

Home infringement: the act of illegally searching or breaking into another person's home without the consent of its owner or manager.

A person who illegally searches another person's home shall face a penalty of 01 year of community sentence.

Hazardous wastes: wastes that are dangerous.

Offences against regulations on hazardous waste management.

Harboring: A place of shelter.

To harbor: to give a home or shelter to someone.

Harboring prostitutes.

Any person who harbors prostitutes shall face a penalty of up to 07 years of imprisonment.

Harassment: the act of annoying or upsetting someone.

Harassment of the people.

SECTION I

Instigation: the action of instigating an action.

Instigation of crimes.

Involuntary crime: the offender is aware of the danger of his/her actions to society but believes that consequences would not occur or could be prevented;

The punishment of the involuntary crime.

Infliction: the action of inflicting something painful on someone.

Deliberate infliction of bodily harm upon other people.

Deliberate infliction of bodily harm by a law enforcement officer in the performance of his/her official duties.

Involuntary infliction of serious property damage.

Infringement upon territory: the act of infringing upon the territory of a country, distorts the national border or commits any other act for the purpose of infringing the territory of such nation.

Any person who infringes upon X's territory, distorts the national border or commits any other act for the purpose of infringing the territory of X shall face a penalty of 05 - 15 years of imprisonment.

Illegal emigration: the act of moving across national borders in a way that violates emigration laws.

Illegal emigration for the purpose of opposing the people's authority.

Terrorism financing: the act of raising or providing money or property in any shape or form to a terrorist or terrorist organization.

Any person who raises or provides money or property in any shape or form to a terrorist or terrorist organization shall face a penalty of 05 - 10 years of imprisonment.

Infringement: an action that breaks a law.

Infringement of national security.

Infringement of copyrights.

Infringement of copyrights and relevant rights.

Infringement of industrial property rights.

Investigation: the action of investigating someone or something.

Activities of investigation must observe the laws.

In peril: in serious and immediate danger.

Failure to assist a person in peril.

Any person who is able to but fails to assist a person in peril shall face a penalty of up to 02 years of imprisonment if such failure results in the death of that person.

Incestuous: involving sexual intercourse between two members of the same family, for example, a daughter and father, a son and mother or a sister and brother.

The offence is of an incestuous nature.

Impoundment: the act of taking and holding something.

Illegal impoundment of property.

Any person who finds or mistakenly receives a piece of property but deliberately fails to return it to its legitimate owner shall face a penalty of up to 02 years' community sentence.

Illegal use of property

Any person who illegally uses a piece of property of another person shall face a penalty of up to 02 years of community sentence.

Incest: sexual relations between two members of the same family, for example, a daughter and father, a son and mother or a sister and brother.

In a drunken state, he commits incest with his daughters.

He commits incest by marrying his cousin.

Illegal transport of goods or money across the border.

Any person who illegally transports goods, domestic currency, foreign currencies, rare metals, gemstones across the border shall face a penalty of up to 02 years of imprisonment.

Insurance fraud: the act of intentionally obtaining a fraudulent outcome from an insurance process.

Any person who colludes with the insured to receive indemnity or insurance payout against the law shall face a penalty of up to 03 years of imprisonment.

Forging documents, falsifying information to reject insurance claims in an occurrence;

Forging documents, falsifying information in the request for indemnity or insurance payout;

Social insurance and unemployment insurance fraud.

Invasive species: a plant or animal species that is not native to a specific location and that tends to cause damage to the environment, or human health.

Any person who illegally imports invasive species or potentially invasive species shall face a penalty of up to 05 years of imprisonment.

Illegal transport of narcotic substances.

Any person who transports narcotic substances for purposes other than manufacturing, trading or possessing narcotic substances shall face a penalty of 01 - 05 years of imprisonment.

Narcotic substance: an addictive drug such as opium, cocaine or heroin or other substance affecting mood or behavior, especially an illegal one.

Illegal production of narcotic substances

Illegal trafficking of narcotic substance

Illegal trading of narcotic substances

Illegal racing: riding an automobiles, motorbike or another motor vehicle over the speed limit that can cause danger to their life and other people on the road.

Organization of illegal racing: to organize a street race which involves automobiles, motorbikes or other motor vehicles.

Any person who illegally organizes a street race which involves automobiles, motorbikes or other motor vehicles shall face a penalty of up to 05 years of imprisonment.

Infiltration: the action of entering or gaining access to the computer network, telecommunications network or electronic device of another person in order to acquire secret information or cause damage.

Illegal infiltration into the computer network, telecommunications network or electronic device of another person.

Any person who deliberately bypasses the warning, hacks the password or firewall to infiltrate another person's computer network, telecommunications network or electronic device in order to steal, change, destroy, fabricate data shall face a penalty of 01 - 03 years of imprisonment.

Illegal collection, possession, exchanging, trading, publishing of information about bank accounts.

Any person who illegally collects, possesses, exchanges, trades, publishes information about other people's bank accounts shall face a penalty of up to 03 years' of imprisonment.

Illegal manufacture, possession, transport, use, trading or appropriation of explosive materials.

Any person who illegally manufactures, possesses, transports, uses, deals in or appropriates explosive materials shall face a penalty of 02 - 07 years of imprisonment.

Illegal manufacture, possession, transport, use or trading of flammable or toxic substances.

Illegal goods are transported or traded across the border.

Issuing an illegal decision.

Any competent person who issues a decision in the knowledge that it is illegal and as a result infringes upon lawful rights and interests of the individual shall face a penalty of up to 03 years of imprisonment.

Insubordination: refusal to obey orders.

Any person who deliberately fails to obey an order given by a competent person shall face a penalty of up to 05 years of imprisonment.

To insult: to speak to or treat someone with disrespect or rudeness.

Insulting companions.

Any person who seriously insults his/her companion at work shall face a penalty of up to 02 years of imprisonment.

Investigation: the act or process of examining a crime.

It is prohibited to disclose investigation secrets perceived during the activities of pleading.

Terminate investigation and lawsuit against suspects.

Inviolability: prohibit violation; secure from violation.

Alimentation of inviolability of residence, privacy, personal secrecy, family secrets, safety and confidentiality of personal mail, telephone and telegraph.

Imprisonment: the act of keeping someone in a prison as a penalty imposed by a court for a certain period of time.

Any person who violates legal regulations on emergency custody of people, imprisonment, investigation, prosecution or adjudication shall be disciplined according to the laws.

Impoundment: placing private property, objects, and documents in the custody of an officer of the law.

Maintenance: the process of preserving something.

Impoundment and maintenance of evidences and materials directly related to the lawsuits.

Interrogation: the process of questioning a person who is arrested or suspected, usually by the police, to seek answers to a crime.

Record statements and interrogation in writing and make other written records upon investigators' inspection and verification of criminal information and criminal investigation.

Impeachment: an attack on the accuracy of witnesses' testimony.

Conduct interrogation, present evidences, documents, items, impeachment, arguments and viewpoints regarding the settlement of the criminal cases.

Identification: the action of proving that a person, object, or photo before the court is the very same that he/she or it is alleged, or charged.

There must be at least three externally identical photos, items, or persons to be identified, except for the identification of corpses.

Involuntary manslaughter: the crime of killing someone unlawfully but unintentionally.

Any person who commits an involuntary manslaughter might face a penalty of up to 03 years of imprisonment.

Illegal abortion: the act of illegally performing an abortion on another person.

Any person who illegally performs an abortion on another person shall face a penalty of up to 03 years' imprisonment.

Offences against regulations of law on food safety and hygiene.

Involuntary disclosure of classified information.

Any person who involuntarily discloses classified information shall face a penalty of up to 02 years of imprisonment.

SECTION K

Kidnapping for ransom: the action of taking another person hostage for ransom.

Any person who takes another person hostage for ransom shall face a penalty of 03 - 05 years of imprisonment.

SECTION J

Justifiable force in self-defense: the act of defending against another person's attack by using force that is reasonably necessary.

Unjustified force in self-defense: the act of defending against another person's attack or infringement by using force that is more than reasonably necessary and not appropriate for the nature and danger of such attack or infringement.

Any person who uses unjustified force in self-defense shall bear criminal responsibility.

Judicial measures.

Confiscation of money and items directly related to the crime; return, repair of property or provision of compensation; offering of public apology; mandatory disease treatment are types of judicial measures.

Judgment: an official decision that is given by a court at the end of a trial.

Passing an illegal judgment.

Any judge or jury member who passes a judgment in the knowledge that it is illegal shall face a penalty of up to 04 years of imprisonment.

Failure to execute a judgment

Failure to serve a judgment

Obstruction of judgment execution

Jury: a group of twelve people who sit in criminal and civil courts to make decisions on matters of facts.

Trial by jury.

Juvenile offenders: offenders who are physiologically immature or undeveloped.

A juvenile offender shall face one of the following punishments for each criminal offence committed:

1. Fine;

2. Warning;

3. Community sentence.

Jail sentence = prison sentence: a term of imprisonment imposed by a court.

The length of the jail sentence is equal to or shorter than the length of the detention of the defendant.

The court president has the authority to decide to suspend prison sentences.

Justifications of the decision not to press criminal charges

A criminal charge shall not be filed in the presence of one of these justifications:

1. Acts do not constitute crime;

2. Criminal acts do not exist;

3. General amnesty has been granted.

SECTION L

Leniency: the state of being lenient/ merciful;

Leniency shall be applied to criminals who show cooperative attitudes; inform on accomplices; express contrition, and voluntarily compensate for the damage they inflict.

Less serious crime: Less serious crime means a crime whose danger to society is not significant.

A person who commits a less serious crime for the first time may only serve a community sentence.

A person convicted of a less serious crime may have the sentence deferred for up to 01 year if required by his/her official duties.

Lack of criminal capacity: A person who suffers from a mental disease or another disease that causes him/her to lose his/her awareness or control of his/her behaviors.

Any person who lack criminal capacity commits an act that is dangerous to society is exempt from criminal responsibility.

Life imprisonment: an indefinite imprisonment imposed upon persons committing extremely serious crimes but not punishable by death.

Life imprisonment shall not be imposed upon offenders under 18 years of age.

Litigants: persons who are involved in a civil legal case.

Litigants include civil plaintiffs, civil defendants and people who incur interests and duties from a criminal lawsuit.

Legal proceeding: a proceeding that permits someone to enter into a lawsuit already in progress.

Institute legal proceedings in court.

Serious breach of legal proceedings.

Legal compliance: the act of complying with rules, regulations or laws.

Legal compliance in investigative activities.

Legal compliance in criminal procedure.

Legal compliance in criminal proceedings.

Lawyer registration card.

A lawyer shall present his lawyer registration card with a certified copy of such and the letter of appointment by the law firm at which such lawyer practices law.

Late appeal.

The filing of a late appeal shall be accepted on condition that the appellant has been obstructed by objective obstacles or force majeure to lodge an appeal within the time limit as defined by the Law.

SECTION M

Mastermind: a person who plans a difficult activity, usually a crime.

That evidence proves that he is the mastermind behind the killing of the president.

Murder: the deliberate and unlawful killing of a person.

Murder of a pregnant woman.

Murder for taking the victim's body parts.

Money laundering: the concealment of the illegal origin of the money or property obtained through the commission of a crime, typically by means of transfers involving foreign banks or legitimate businesses.

Any person who directly or indirectly participates in financial transactions or other transactions to conceal the illegal origin of the money or property obtained through his/her commission of a crime shall face a penalty of 01 - 05 years' imprisonment.

His father was convicted of money laundering and tax evasion.

Misprision: the act of failing to report a crime despite knowing such crime is being prepared, being carried out or has been carried out.

Any person who knows about the preparation or commission of a crime but fails to report such crime shall bear criminal responsibility for misprision.

Mandatory supervision: Mandatory supervision means forcing a person sentenced to imprisonment to reside, work and live within a defined area under the supervision of the local authority and local people.

Mandatory supervision shall be imposed upon persons committing crimes against national security, dangerous recidivism.

Mandatory disease treatment: the act of sending a person who commits an act dangerous to society to a specialized medical facility for mandatory treatment.

Mandatory disease treatment is a type of judicial measure.

Make rectification: to remedy; to correct something.

Peter will be dismissed unless he makes rectification within a specified time limit.

Manslaughter: the crime of unintentionally killing a person.

Manslaughter under provocation.

Manslaughter by a law enforcement officer in the performance of his/her official duties.

Molestation = obscenity: sexual abuse or assault of a person, especially a woman or a child.

Molestation of a person under 16.

Any person who molests a person aged under 16 for purposes other than sexual intercourse or other sexual activities shall face a penalty of up to 03 years of imprisonment.

Mitigating factors: factors that can cause punishment to decrease.

The following circumstances are considered mitigating factors:

a) The crime is committed under provocation caused by the victim's illegal acts;

b) The criminal offender has prevented or reduced the harm caused by the crime;

c) The criminal offender voluntarily pays damages, makes rectification, or relieves the consequences.

Mandate of investigation: an order of investigation from an appellate court directing a lower court to take action.

An investigation authority shall mandate another investigation authority to conduct certain investigations.

SECTION N

Nature of cassation procedure.

The cassation procedure reviews a Court's effective sentences and rulings under protest upon the exposure of a serious breach of law in the settlement of the case.

Nature of reopening procedure.

The reopening procedure reviews a Court's effective sentences and rulings under protest upon the exposure of new facts that may alter the fundamentals of such sentences and rulings, given that the said Court had no knowledge of such facts when passing its judgments and decisions.

SECTION O

Obstinacy = stubbornness.

His obstinacy was irritating.

Offender: someone who is guilty of a crime/ commits an illegal act.

The criminal offender shall be exempt from criminal responsibility if he/ she is granted a general amnesty.

The offender must return the appropriated property to its lawful owner.

Organized crime: Organized crime is a form of complicity in which a group of professional criminals cooperate closely in committing a crime.

Organized crime is considered an aggravating factor.

Offences against regulations on medical examination, and medical treatment.

Any person who violates regulations of law on medical examination, or medical treatment shall face a penalty of 01 - 05 years of imprisonment.

Old and weak people

Community sentence shall not be applied to pregnant women, women raising children under 06 months of age, people having fatal diseases, old and weak people, and people having severe disabilities or extremely severe disabilities.

Organization of child marriage

Any person who organizes a marriage entered into by a person under the marriageable age shall face a penalty of up to 02 years of community sentence.

Offences against regulations on land use.

Any person who appropriates land, transfers land use right or uses land against regulations of law on management and use of land might face a penalty of up to 02 years of imprisonment.

Opium: a drug made from the seeds of a poppy that is used to control pain or sometimes used by people as an illegal drug.

Dried opium poppy fruits.

Fresh opium poppy fruits.

Solid narcotic substances.

Obstruction: the action of obstructing with an obstacle or obstacles.

Obstruction of road traffic.

Obstruction of rail traffic.

Obstruction of waterway traffic.

Obstruction of air traffic.

Obstruction or disturbance of computer networks, telecommunications networks or electronic devices.

Any person who deletes, damages or changes a software program or electronic data or illegally obstructs the transmission of data of a computer network, telecommunications network or an electronic device shall face a penalty of 02 years of imprisonment.

Obstruction of conscription.

Any person who deliberately obstructs conscription, enlistment, military training order shall face a penalty of up to 02 years of imprisonment.

Oral argument: The spoken legal statements and presentation by the attorneys before a court in defense of a client's case.

Oral arguments in court.

The judge shall not restrict the time for oral arguments and shall allow Procurators, defendants, defense counsels to argue and state all viewpoints.

Obligatory medical treatment measures.

The head of the procuracy has the duties and authority to decide to enforce or terminate obligatory medical treatment measures.

Temporary suspension: A temporary stop of a right by law.

The temporary suspension and resumption of the processing of criminal information.

SECTION P

Punish: to impose a penalty on someone who commits a crime.

To punish crimes.

Piracy: the act of attacking and robbing ships at sea.

Any person who robs or destroys property on a ship, aircraft or another maritime vehicle shall face a penalty of 05 - 10 years of imprisonment.

Procedural expenses.

Procedural expenses include Court fee, procedural expenditure and administrative fees.

Preparation for crimes: Preparation for a crime means finding, preparing tools, equipment or other conditions for the crime.

A person who prepares for extremely serious crimes shall bear criminal responsibility.

Perpetrator: someone who actually commits a crime (an illegal act).

Helper: someone who helps or gives assistance, support, etc. to another in committing a crime.

An accomplice means an organizer, perpetrator, instigator or abettor.

Prosecution: the action of prosecuting someone.

Time limit for criminal prosecution.

The procuracy exercises the right of prosecution and oversees legal compliance in criminal procedure.

Prohibition from holding certain positions or doing certain works.

Prohibition from holding certain positions or doing certain works shall be imposed when the convict is deemed to cause harm to society if he/she is allowed to hold the positions or do the works.

Prohibition from residence: prohibition from residence means preventing the person sentenced to imprisonment from temporarily or permanently residing in certain administrative divisions.

The offender might face prohibition from residence for 02 - 04 years.

Permanent shutdown: Permanent shutdown means termination of an organization in one or some fields in which such organization causes damage or possibly harms life, health of many people, causes environmental emergencies or negatively impact social security or order and the damage cannot be repaired.

Permanent shutdown is a type of primary sentence.

Public order crime: criminal acts that are considered as harmful to the public good and moral values.

Public safety: refers to the protection of the general public.

Infringement upon public safety, public order.

People having fatal diseases

People having severe disabilities or extremely severe disabilities.

Women raising children under 06 months of age.

Provocation: an action that makes someone angry, annoyed or sometimes even violent, especially deliberately.

Manslaughter under provocation.

Deliberate infliction of bodily harm upon others under provocation.

Probation: the release of an offender from detention, subject to a period of time when a criminal behaves well and not commit any more crimes.

In consideration of the offender's records and mitigating factors, the Court might give probation of 1 - 5 years and request the convict to fulfill certain obligations during this period.

During the probation period, the person put on probation shall be supervised and educated by the organization or agency for which he/she works or the local authority.

Possession and transport of banned goods.

Any person who possesses or transports goods banned from trading, or using shall face a penalty of 02 years of imprisonment.

Property auction: a public event at which property are sold to the highest bidder.

Any person who colludes with other people to decrease or increase prices during a property auction shall face a penalty of 02 years of imprisonment.

Persuading or inciting others to use narcotic substances.

Any person who persuades, incites or persuades another person to illegally use narcotic substances shall face a penalty of up to 06 years of imprisonment.

Psychotropic drugs: drugs that are capable of affecting the mind, emotions, and behavior.

Any person who violates regulations on export and import of psychotropic drugs shall face a penalty of 01 - 05 years' imprisonment.

Any person who illegally drills, digs, cuts, buries road traffic works shall face a penalty of up to 03 years of imprisonment.

Pornographic materials: materials that depict erotic behavior and are intended to cause sexual excitement.

Distribution pornographic materials.

Any person who makes, duplicates, or publishes books, magazines, films, pictures or that contain pornographic contents for the purpose of distributing them shall face a penalty of up to 03 years' imprisonment.

Prostitutes: persons, particularly women, who engage in sexual activity for payment.

Any person who harbors prostitutes shall face a penalty of up to 05 years' imprisonment.

Procuring: the action of encouraging or assisting the prostitution of others.

Any person who encourages or assists the prostitution of others shall face a penalty of up to 02 years of imprisonment.

Prosecution: the act of holding a trial against someone who is accused of a crime to see if he/she is guilty.

The procuracy exercises the right of prosecution and oversees legal compliance in criminal procedure.

Presumption: a conclusion based upon a general rule and not upon the facts or evidence.

Presumption of innocence: a defendant is innocent until proven guilty.

An accused person is deemed innocent until his guilt is evidenced.

Prosecutors: a person who prosecutes another for a crime before a court; prosecuting attorney.

The Court is responsible for supporting defendants, defense counsels, investigators, and prosecutors to perform all of their rights and obligations.

Pleading: a formal written statement of a party's claims or defenses on behalf of his/her client to another party's claims in a legal proceeding.

Defense counsels are able to perform activities of pleading on behalf of his/her clients.

Pronouncement of judgment: a declaration of a verdict or decision by a court.

The presiding judge shall read the sentence document.

A criminal trial commences with the charge and ends at the pronouncement of judgment.

Parole: the conditional release of a convicted criminal defendant before he/she completes his/her sentence.

Procedures for parole.

The convict's letter of application for parole, including his undertakings to obey the laws and perform mandatory duties of the parole.

SECTION R

Rape: to use violence or threatens to use violence to have sexual intercourse with the victim against their will.

Any person who uses violence or threatens to use violence or takes advantage of the victim's defenselessness to have non-consensual sexual intercourse shall face a penalty of 03 - 07 years' imprisonment.

Raping people under 16 years of age.

Recognition of voices.

There must be at least three voices in similar timbre and loudness to be recognized.

Radioactive substances: substances that emit ionizing radiation.

Any person who discharges into the environment wastewater that contains radioactive substances that cause contamination shall face a penalty of 01 - 05 years' imprisonment.

Illegal manufacture, possession, transport, use, spreading, trading or appropriation of radioactive substances or nuclear materials.

Robbery: to use violence, threat of immediate violence to obtain someone's property.

Any person who uses violence, threat of immediate violence or commits other acts that render another person unable to resist in order to obtain his/her property shall face a penalty of 04 — 9 years of imprisonment.

Rebellion: the act of engaging in armed activities or using organized force to act against the people's government.

Any person who engages in armed activities or uses organized force to act against the people's government face a penalty of 05 - 15 years of imprisonment.

Reconciliation: the action of reconciling.

Reconciliation shall be applied to a juvenile offender aged from 16 to under 18 commits a less serious crime or serious crime.

Restoration: the act of restoring/ the action of repairing or renewing something.

Compulsory restoration of original state.

The damage is too great for restoration.

Recidivism: the tendency of a convicted criminal to continue to commit crimes even after he/she has been punished.

Recidivism is a situation in which a person who has an unspent conviction for the same offence and deliberately commits a very serious crime.

Reprimand: a severe, or formal reproof.

A reprimand shall be issued against a juvenile offender in order to help him/her be aware of his/her criminal act and its consequences for the society.

Conditional parole: the conditional release of a person from prison before their period in prison is finished, with the agreement that they will behave well.

Rebellion: the act of engaging in armed activities or using organized force to act against the people's government.

Any person who engages in armed activities or uses organized force to act against the people's government shall face a penalty of 12 - 20 years of imprisonment, life imprisonment or death.

Relief: assistance, especially in the form of money, food, or clothing given to people who are in special need or difficulty.

Offences against regulations on distribution of relief money or relief goods.

Rehabilitation: the action of restoring someone to health after addiction through training and therapy.

The offence is committed against a person undergoing rehabilitation.

Residential confinement: a preventive measure that may apply to suspects and defendants who have a definite place of residence and records assuring their presence in court as per subpoena.

Presiding judges are entitled to issue residential confinement orders.

The length of time of residential confinement shall not exceed the time of investigation, prosecution or adjudication according to the Law.

SECTION S

Serious crime: a serious crime means a crime whose danger to society is significant.

The time limit for criminal prosecution of serious crimes is 10 years.

Very serious crime: Very serious crime means a crime whose danger to society is great.

Fine shall be imposed against people who commit very serious crimes against the law on economics, environment, public order, and public safety.

Sexual abuse: someone who uses trickery to make a child who is his care-dependent or a person in extreme need to reluctantly have sexual intercourse.

Sexual abuse of people from 13 to under 16 years of age.

Self-defense: the act of defending self when being physically attacked.

Justifiable force in self-defense.

Unjustified force in self-defense.

Suspension of operation: Suspension of operation means suspension of an organization in one or some fields in which such organization harms human life, health, the environment, social security or order and the damage can be repaired in reality.

Suspension of operation of vehicles.

Suspension: the action of suspending someone or something for a while.

Suspension of operation.

The offender has made reparation in an effort to atone for the crime during the suspension period.

Smuggling: the crime of importing or exporting goods or people secretly contrary to the law.

Any person who conducts deals in the illegal goods across the border shall face a penalty of 1 - 3 years of imprisonment.

Sabotage: deliberately destroy, or damage something.

Sabotage of technical facilities.

Sabotage of peace, crimes against humanity and war crimes.

Sexual slavery: the state of being raped, sexually abused, or forced to work as a prostitute.

Slander: the act of fabricating information or spreading false information to harm another person's reputation.

He was found guilty of slander against his employers.

Spreading dangerous infectious diseases in human.

Any person who brings or allows another entity to bring animals, plants or products that are likely to transmit dangerous infectious diseases in human shall face a penalty of 01 - 04 years of imprisonment.

Strong stimulants: substances that raise high levels of physiological or nervous activity in the body.

Crimes committed under the influence of alcohol or other strong stimulants.

Spreading software programs harmful to computer networks, telecommunications networks or electronic devices.

Any person who deliberately spreads a software program that is harmful to a computer network, telecommunications network or an electronic device shall face a penalty of up to 02 years of imprisonment.

Superstition: an excessively credulous belief or practice in and reverence for supernatural beings.

Practicing superstitions.

Any person who practices fortune-telling, witchcraft or other types of superstitions shall face a penalty of up to 03 years of imprisonment.

Surrender: a perpetrator, after exposed, voluntarily turning himself/herself in and giving statements on his/her offences to competent authorities.

Sentence enforcement: Making sure a court's sentence is properly followed.

Records of legal proceedings, investigation, prosecution, adjudication, and sentence enforcement are lawful evidences.

Subpoena: a written legal order telling someone to appear in court on a certain day to give testimony or evidence.

Defendants must have the duty to appear in court as per the Court's subpoena.

Sources of evidences.

Evidences are collected and determined from these sources:

a) Statements, presentations;

b) Exhibits;

c) Electronic data;

A search of body, residence, workplace, area, vehicle.

A search of body, residence, workplace, area, vehicle shall only be permissible in the presence of justifications showing the existence of criminal documents, instruments, property, items obtained by crime.

Start of trial: the beginning of the trial.

The presiding judge starts the trial and utters the decision to hear the case.

SECTION T

To atone: to make reparation or compensation for something bad.

The offender has made reparation in an effort to atone for the crime. This is considered a mitigating factor.

Terrorism: the act of using violence and threats to harm other people's life or destroy property of another organization or individual to bring terror to the public.

Terrorism to oppose the people's government.

Terrorism aimed to oppose the people's authority.

Any person who uses violence and threats to harm other people's life or destroy the property of another organization or individual to bring terror to the public shall face a penalty of 18 years of imprisonment, life imprisonment or death.

Taking hostages: the act of taking someone hostage and threatens to kill, hurt him/ her or detains the hostage to force a nation, territory, or individual to act or not to act as a condition for releasing the hostage.

Any person who takes another person hostage shall face a penalty of 02 - 07 years of imprisonment.

Trial: a formal examination of evidence in a law court in order to decide guilt in a case of criminal proceedings.

A judge has the obligation to examine case files prior to the start of a trial.

To traffic = to transport: the movement of something.

Illegal trafficking of goods or money across the border.

Tax evasion: the illegal nonpayment or underpayment of tax by individuals, corporations, and trusts.

He pleaded guilty to mail fraud and tax evasion.

To incite: to encourage, or urge someone to do something.

To aid: to help, assist, or support someone to achieve something.

Inciting or aiding another to commit suicide.

Any person inciting, aiding, persuading another to commit suicide shall face a penalty of up to 02 years of imprisonment.

Tax registration.

Failure to submit the application for tax registration.

Tax declaration.

Failure to submit tax declaration.

To forge: to produce a copy or imitation of a document for the purpose of deception.

Forging medical records or prescriptions.

Forging documents, health insurance cards in order to illegally obtain health insurance benefits.

Forging an office holder's signature.

The influence of alcohol with blood or breath alcohol content.

The offender is under the influence of alcohol with blood or breath alcohol content above the limit.

Torture: the act of causing great physical or mental pain as a punishment in order to force someone to do or say something.

Any person who uses torture or brutally treats or insults another person in any shape or form shall face a penalty of up to 02 years of imprisonment.

To swap = to exchange: to give something and receive something else in exchange.

Swapping a person under 01 year of age.

To uphold = to defend; support.

To uphold justice.

To arrest: to take or keep a person in lawful custody.

No person is arrested without a Court's warrant or Procuracy's decision or approval.

To detain: to keep or hold someone in custody.

Temporarily detained.

To denounce: to accuse or inform against someone publicly.

Individuals are permitted to file complaints or denouncement in criminal procedure.

Competent authorities and persons must receive and settle complaints and denouncements in timely and lawful manners.

To summon: to call or notify someone to appear in a court of law.

To interrogate: to question a suspect to gather information from him/her.

Summon and interrogate suspects.

To redress: to remedy.

To annul: to destroy; to put an end to.

Decide to redress or annul baseless and illegitimate decisions.

To vacate = to annul: to destroy; to put an end to.

Decide to redress or vacate unfounded and illegal decisions.

Temporary detainees.

Temporary detainees are held in emergency captivity or arrested for criminal acts in flagrante or wanted notices or those confessing or surrendering and facing existing orders of temporary detainment.

Trial preparation.

Time limit for trial preparation.

The extension of the time limit for trial preparation.

To halt: to bring to a stop; to put a stop to something.

A temporary halt to trial.

The court shall halt the trial in case evidences, documents or items must be verified or supplemented outside the court.

The appellant: someone who requests or asks a higher court for a reversal of the decision or verdict of a lower court.

The appellant lodges an appeal to the court that conducted the first instance trial.

If the appellant submits the written appeal in court, the entry date of the appeal shall be fixed upon the Court's receipt of the written appeal.

Time limit for appeal.

The time limit for appeal against a first-instance court's judgments is 15 days upon the pronouncement of such judgments.

The remedy of reprimand.

The head of investigation authorities, procuracies or the Trial panel decides to implement the remedy of reprimand against the juvenile criminals who are exempt from criminal liabilities but is eligible for reprimand.

SECTION U

Unexpected events: events that cannot be foreseen or have to be foreseen.

Any person who commits an act that results in harmful consequences is exempt from criminal responsibility if such consequences cannot be foreseen or have to be foreseen.

Urgent circumstance: An urgent circumstance is a circumstance in which there is no other choice but an amount of damage has to be inflicted in order to prevent a greater damage.

The act of inflicting damage in an urgent circumstance does not constitute a criminal offense.

A criminal offense: an illegal action that is punishable by law.

He was convicted of a criminal offense.

Unjustified force in self-defense: Unjustified force in self-defense means the use of force which is more than reasonably necessary and not appropriate for the nature and danger to society posed by the infringement.

Any person who uses unjustified force in self-defense shall bear criminal responsibility.

Usury: the action of lending money at unreasonably high rates of interest.

Usury in civil transactions.

SECTION V

Voluntary termination commission of crimes: means someone's voluntarily stopping committing the crime without anything stopping him/her from committing such crime.

Any person who voluntarily terminates the commission of a crime is exempt from criminal responsibility.

Violation: the act of violating something, especially a law, or agreement.

Violations against regulations on competition.

Violations against regulations on survey, exploration and extraction of natural resources.

Violations against regulations on forest extraction and protection.

Violations against regulations on management and protection of wild animals.

Violations against regulations on environmental emergency prevention, response and relief.

Violations against regulations of law on occupational safety, occupational hygiene and safety in crowded areas.

Any person who violates regulations of law on occupational safety, occupational hygiene or safety in crowded areas shall face a penalty of 01 - 05 years of imprisonment.

Vandalism: deliberate destruction of property.

Any person who deliberately destroy another person's property shall face a penalty of up to 02 years of imprisonment.

SECTION W

Warning: Warning is imposed upon persons who commit less serious crimes and have multiple mitigating factors but are not eligible for exemption from sentence.

Any person who involuntarily inflicts 31% - 60% WPI to another person shall receive a warning, or face a penalty of up to 02 years of community sentence.

Water sources: sources of water that are potentially useful to humans.

The illegal profit from survey, exploration, extraction of water resources.

Water-borne vehicles: vehicles that are used to travel on water.

Any person who allows another person who does not have an appropriate license, certificate or qualification to operate water-borne vehicles might face a penalty of up to 02 years' imprisonment.

Offences against regulations on control of water-borne vehicles.

Offences against regulations on airplane operation.

Offences against regulations of maintenance, repair, management of traffic works.

Warranty: A guarantee given on the performance of a certain thing.

Warranty of the effect of Court's judgments and rulings.

Wanted notice: a public announcement by a competent agency that they desire to arrest someone.

Persons held in emergency custody or arrested for wanted notices are entitled to defend themselves or be defended.

CONCLUSION

Thank you again for downloading this book on *"Criminal Law Vocabulary In Use: Master 400+ Essential Criminal Law Terms And Phrases Explained With Examples In 10 Minutes A Day."* and reading all the way to the end. I'm extremely grateful.

If you know of anyone else who may benefit from the essential Criminal Law terms and phrases explained with examples that are revealed in this book, please help me inform them of this book. I would greatly appreciate it.

Finally, if you enjoyed this book and feel that it has added value to your work and study in any way, please take a couple of minutes to share your thoughts and post a REVIEW on Amazon. Your feedback will help me to continue to write other books of Law topic that helps you get the best results. Furthermore, if you write a simple REVIEW with positive words for this book on Amazon, you can help hundreds or perhaps thousands of other readers who may want to improve their legal vocabulary so that they could get the greatest achievements in work and study. Like you, they worked hard for every penny they spend on books. With the information and recommendation you provide, they would be more likely to take action right away. We really look forward to reading your review.

Thanks again for your support and good luck!

If you enjoy my book, please write a POSITIVE REVIEW on Amazon.

-- Johnny Chuong --

CHECK OUT OTHER BOOKS

Go here to check out other related books that might interest you:

Legal Vocabulary In Use: Master 600+ Essential Legal Terms And Phrases Explained In 10 Minutes A Day

http://www.amazon.com/dp/B01L0FKXPU

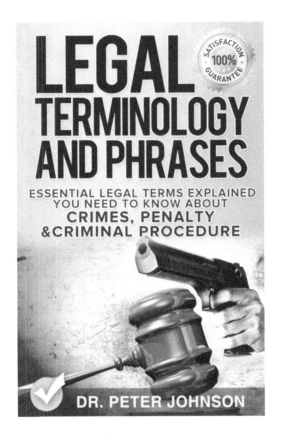

Legal Terminology And Phrases: Essential Legal Terms Explained You Need To Know About Crimes, Penalty And Criminal Procedure

http://www.amazon.com/dp/B01L5EB54Y

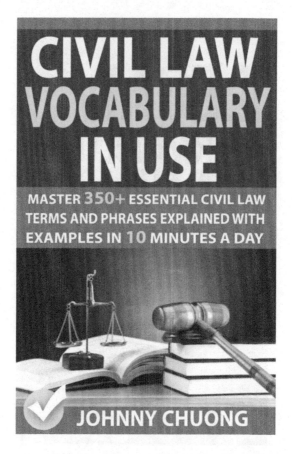

Civil Law Vocabulary In Use: Master 350+ Essential Civil Law Terms
And Phrases Explained With Examples In 10 Minutes A Day.

https://www.amazon.com/dp/B0781TQWGV

Ielts Writing Task 2 Samples : Over 450 High-Quality Model Essays for Your Reference to Gain a High Band Score 8.0+ In 1 Week (Box set) https://www.amazon.com/dp/B077BYQLPG

Ielts Academic Writing Task 1 Samples: Over 450 High Quality Samples for Your Reference to Gain a High Band Score 8.0+ In 1 Week (Box set) https://www.amazon.com/dp/B077CC5ZG4

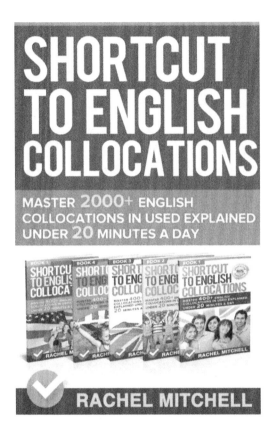

Shortcut To English Collocations: Master 2000+ English Collocations In Used Explained Under 20 Minutes A Day (5 books in 1 Box set)

https://www.amazon.com/dp/B06W2P6S22

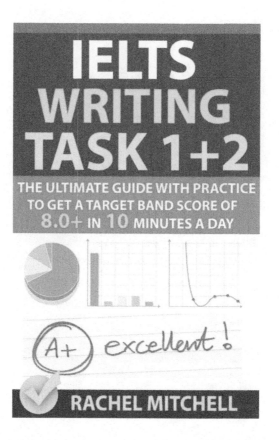

IELTS Writing Task 1 + 2: The Ultimate Guide with Practice to Get a Target Band Score of 8.0+ In 10 Minutes a Day

https://www.amazon.com/dp/B075DFYPG6

IELTS Speaking Strategies: The Ultimate Guide With Tips, Tricks, And Practice On How To Get A Target Band Score Of 8.0+ In 10 Minutes A Day.

https://www.amazon.com/dp/B075JCW65G

Shortcut To Ielts Writing: The Ultimate Guide To Immediately Increase Your Ielts Writing Scores.

https://www.amazon.com/dp/B01JV7EQGG

Common English Mistakes Explained With Examples: Over 600
Mistakes Almost Students Make and How to Avoid Them in Less
Than 5 Minutes A Day

https://www.amazon.com/dp/B072PXVHNZ

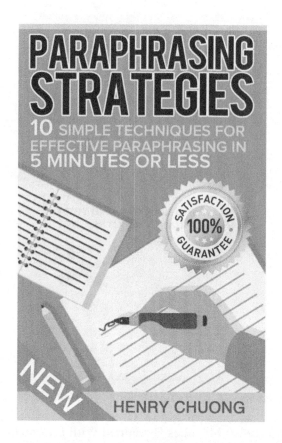

Paraphrasing Strategies: 10 Simple Techniques For Effective Paraphrasing In 5 Minutes Or Less

https://www.amazon.com/dp/B071DFG27Q

Productivity Secrets For Students: The Ultimate Guide To Improve
Your Mental Concentration, Kill Procrastination, Boost Memory And
Maximize Productivity In Study

http://www.amazon.com/dp/B01JS52UT6

Made in the USA
Las Vegas, NV
23 January 2024

84739796R00059